CROCK POT

COOKBOOK

For Singles

Easy, Delicious, and Time-Saving Recipes for
Helping Busy Singles Create Flavorful and
Satisfying Meals

BELL QUINTANA

TABLE OF CONTENT

INTRODUCTION

A friend of mine, Stephanie had always loved the idea of cooking, but as a busy single professional, the reality often fell short of her culinary dreams. She yearned for excellent, cooked dinners but, due to her tight schedule, had to settle for takeaway or boring, repetitive dishes.

One day, I gifted her the recipes and instructions in this cookbook, Skeptical yet hopeful, she decided to give it a try. And indeed she was captivated by the recipes' simplicity and the promise of excellent dinners with little to no effort.

She began with the Honey Garlic Chicken—a mere five ingredients, all easily found in her pantry. Stephanie's scepticism gave way to excitement as the aroma filled her flat that evening. She was taken aback by the first bite of succulent chicken brimming with savoury sweetness. She had effortlessly crafted a gourmet-worthy entrée.

With newfound enthusiasm, Stephanie delved deeper, trying various recipes. Each one proved to be a revelation—a symphony of flavors that didn't require hours in the kitchen or complex cooking skills. The Beef Chili, Lemon-Garlic Butter Salmon, and Berry Cobbler became staples in her repertoire.

But it wasn't just about the recipes. My gift to her became her guide, introducing her to the art of slow cooking and offering valuable tips for cooking for one. Stephanie discovered the joy of batch cooking, turning leftovers into creative, delectable meals. She discovered the art of freezing and reheating meals, making her evenings free of stress and her lunches at work enviable.

That simple gift didn't just teach her recipes; it transformed her relationship with cooking. She started inviting friends over for cozy dinners, proudly presenting dishes she once thought were beyond her reach. It wasn't just about the recipes; it was about rediscovering the joy of cooking in the midst of a demanding schedule.

Getting Started with Your Crock Pot

Your crock pot is a useful kitchen tool that may help you streamline meal preparation and improve your cooking skills. Whether you're new to using a crock pot or an experienced user, the following tips will help you get the most out of this fantastic appliance:

1. Familiarize Yourself with Your Crock Pot:

Read the instruction manual: Learn about the features and settings of your unique crock pot model.

Understand the sizes and settings: Crock pots come in a variety of sizes and heat settings. Knowing this can help you adapt recipes to the capacity of your pot and determine the appropriate cooking time and temperature.

2. Prepping Your Crock Pot:

It should be well cleaned: Before and after each use, thoroughly clean the crock pot, lid, and other removable parts.

Seasoning: Some crock pots might benefit from seasoning the stoneware before use, according to instructions in the manual. This contributes to nonstick qualities and flavour retention.

3. Selecting Recipes:

Start simple: Begin with simple, straightforward dishes to become acquainted with the cooking method of your crock pot.

Adapt recipes: Select recipes that are appropriate for your taste preferences and quantity quantities. Many recipes can be adapted to serve a single person in a reduced portion.

4. Gathering Ingredients:

Embrace the beauty of 5-ingredient meals by minimising shopping lists and preparation time.

Ensure that the ingredients are fresh: For the finest flavours, use fresh, high-quality ingredients. When frozen goods are called for in a recipe, don't be afraid to use them.

5. Cooking Preparation:

Follow stacking instructions: To achieve consistent cooking, some recipes may need layering ingredients in a specified order.

Cooking times should be adjusted as needed to get a sense of how your crock pot operates. Remember that each model can differ somewhat.

6. Precautions for Safety:

Handle with caution: Always use caution when handling the crock pot and its contents, especially when they are hot.

While crock pots are designed for unattended cooking, it's a good idea to check on them every now and then, especially when trying a new recipe.

7. Experiment and Have Fun:

Be daring: Once you're comfortable, don't be afraid to experiment with flavours, spices, and ingredient combinations.

Take pleasure in the process: Enjoy the ease and convenience of slow cooking, as well as the anticipation of your home filling with delicious aromas.

Following these steps will rapidly teach you how to use your crock pot to make tasty, hassle-free meals that suit your taste and lifestyle.

Tips for Cooking for One

Cooking for yourself can be a rewarding and pleasurable activity. Here are some helpful hints for making the most of your cooking efforts while cooking for one:

1) Plan Your Meals:

Make a plan: Plan out your week's meals to reduce waste and provide diversity.
Use batch cooking: Prepare larger portions and freeze individual servings for quick and easy meals in the future.

2) Shop Smart:

Purchase in smaller quantities: To avoid food spoilage, buy fresh produce and perishables in lesser quantities.
Consider frozen and canned items: These can be lifesavers for single servings, providing flexibility without wasting food.

3) Embrace Versatility:

Choose ingredients that are versatile: Choose components like poultry, grains, or veggies that may be utilised in numerous dishes throughout the week.
Repurpose leftovers: Change up yesterday's dinner by adding new ingredients or using it as a base for another dish.

4) Use Kitchen Tools Wisely:

Invest in modest kitchen appliances: To minimise cooking surplus portions, use smaller pans, pots, and tools designed for single servings.
Make use of the freezer: Freeze leftovers or additional portions in freezer-friendly containers for future meals.

5) Experiment and Simplify:

Experiment with new recipes: To keep meals interesting, try new cuisines or cooking techniques.
To reduce food waste, choose recipes with fewer ingredients or those that can be easily scaled down.

6) Mindful Cooking:

Take pleasure in the process: Cooking for oneself may be both therapeutic and pleasurable. Take advantage of the opportunity to experiment and enjoy the cooking experience.
Exercise portion control: To avoid overcooking and to maintain a balanced diet, pay attention to portion sizes.

7) Mindset Change:

Treat yourself: Consider cooking for one as an opportunity to treat yourself to your favourite foods or to try new culinary experiences.
Enjoy meals consciously: While dining alone, create a relaxing atmosphere by lighting candles, playing music, or simply taking your time to enjoy your food.

8) Sharing and Community:

Invite friends over for shared meals, or consider joining cooking groups or community activities to meet others who have similar interests.
To reduce waste and spread kindness, share excess servings with neighbours, friends, or local shelters if you prepare in bulk.
Cooking for one may be a rewarding experience that allows you to experiment with flavours, try new recipes, and adapt to your specific preferences. By following these guidelines, you'll find that cooking for oneself can be both convenient and pleasant.

CHAPTER 1

Soups and Stews

Here are five simple and delicious recipes for soups and stews.

1.1 Hearty Chicken Noodle Soup

Ingredients:

- 1 skinless, boneless chicken breast
- 4 cups of chicken broth
- 1 cup carrots, chopped
- 1 cup celery, chopped
- 1 cup uncooked egg noodles

Preparation:

1. In the crock pot, place the chicken breast, chicken broth, carrots, and celery.

2. Cook for 6-8 hours on low or 3-4 hours on high, or until the chicken is cooked.

3. Remove the chicken and shred it with two forks before returning it to the pot.

4. Add the uncooked egg noodles to the pot and cook for 20-30 minutes, or until the noodles are soft.

5. Before serving, season with salt and pepper to taste.

1.2 Beef and Vegetable Stew

Ingredients:

- 1 pound cubed stew meat
- 3 cups of beef broth
- Two (2) cups of diced potatoes
- 1 cup finely chopped onions
- 1 cup carrots, sliced

Preparation:

1. In the crock pot, add the stew beef, beef broth, potatoes, onions, and carrots.

2. Cook for 7-9 hours on low or 4-6 hours on high, or until the beef is tender.

3. Before serving, season with salt and pepper to taste.

1.3 Lentil and Tomato Soup

Ingredients:

- One (1) cup rinsed dried lentils
- Four (4) cups vegetable broth
- 1 can diced tomatoes (14 oz)
- 1 cup chopped onions
- 2 minced garlic cloves

Preparation:

1. In the crock pot, combine lentils, vegetable broth, chopped tomatoes (with juice), onions, and garlic.

2. Cook for 6-8 hours on low or 3-4 hours on high, or until the lentils are cooked.

3. Before serving, season with salt and pepper to taste.

1.4 Split Pea Soup

Ingredients:

- One (1) pound dried split peas, rinsed
- 6 cup veggie broth or water
- One (1) cup diced ham
- One (1) cup diced carrots
- 1 cup diced onions

Preparation:

1. In the crock pot, combine split peas, water or vegetable broth, diced ham, carrots, and onions.

2. Cook for 8-10 hours on low or 4-6 hours on high, until the peas are tender and the soup thickens.

3. Before serving, season with salt and pepper to taste.

1.5 Creamy Potato Soup

Ingredients:

- Four cups of diced potatoes
- Four cups of broth (chicken or vegetarian)
- 1 cup chopped onions
- 1 cup cheddar cheese, shredded
- One cup of heavy cream or milk

Preparation:

1. In the crock pot, combine the diced potatoes, broth, onions, and shredded cheddar cheese.

2. Cook for 6-8 hours on low or 3-4 hours on high, or until the potatoes are soft.

3. Add the heavy cream or milk and simmer for another 30 minutes.

4. Before serving, season with salt and pepper to taste.

These recipes include a variety of savoury soups and stews with few ingredients, making them ideal for individuals cooking for themselves and looking for fantastic, easy-to-make meals.

CHAPTER 2

One-Pot Meal

2.1 BBQ Pulled Pork

Ingredients:

- 2 pounds pork shoulder or buttocks
- 1 cup barbecue sauce
- a half-cup apple cider vinegar
- 1/4 cup brown sugar
- For serving, hamburger buns

Preparation:

1. Place your pork shoulder in the crock pot.

2. Combine the BBQ sauce, apple cider vinegar, and brown sugar in a mixing bowl, then pour the mixture on top of the pork.

3. Cook for 8-10 hours on low or 4-6 hours on high, or until the pork is soft and readily shreds with a fork.

4. Shred the pork with two forks and combine it with the sauce in the crock pot.

5. Put the pulled pork on hamburger buns and serve.

2.2 Italian Sausage with Peppers

Ingredients:

- 1 pound sweet or spicy Italian sausage links
- 2 sliced bell peppers (green, red, or yellow)
- One (sliced) onion
- 1 can (14 oz) of crushed tomatoes
- 2 minced garlic cloves
- Italian seasoning, to taste

Preparation:

1. In the crock pot, combine the Italian sausage, bell peppers, onion, crushed tomatoes, garlic, and Italian seasoning.

2. Cook for 6-8 hours on low or 3-4 hours on high, or until the sausage is fully cooked and the vegetables are soft.

3. Serve the sausage and peppers on their own or alongside pasta or crusty bread.

2.3 Honey Garlic Chicken

Ingredients:

- Four (4) skinless boneless chicken thighs
- A quarter-cup of soy sauce
- One tablespoon of honey
- 2 minced garlic cloves
- 1 teaspoon of ketchup
- Optional garnishes: sesame seeds and chopped green onions

Preparation:

1. Place the chicken thighs in your crock pot.

2. Combine the soy sauce, honey, minced garlic, and ketchup in a mixing bowl. Pour the mixture over the chicken.

3. Cook for 4-6 hours on low or 2-3 hours on high, or until the chicken is cooked through.

4. If preferred, garnish with sesame seeds and chopped green onions. Serve with rice or veggies.

2.4 Veggie Ratatouille

Ingredients:

- 2 sliced zucchini
- Two (2) sliced yellow squash
- One (1) eggplant, cubed
- One (1) sliced onion
- 2 chopped bell peppers (any colour you prefer)
- 2 minced garlic cloves
- 1 can diced tomatoes (14 oz)
- Italian seasoning (to taste)

Preparation:

1. In the crock pot, combine all of the sliced and diced vegetables, garlic, diced tomatoes, and Italian spice.

2. Cook for 6-8 hours on low or 3-4 hours on high, or until the vegetables are soft.

3. Before serving, season with salt and pepper to taste. This meal is great as a side dish or over rice or pasta.

2.5 Beef Chili

Ingredients:

- 1 pound beef, ground
- 1 can (14 oz) washed and drained kidney beans
- 1 can chopped tomatoes (14 oz)
- 1 (chopped) onion
- 2 minced garlic cloves

- Two (2) tablespoons chili powder
- 1 teaspoon cumin
- Season with salt and pepper to taste.
- Toppings: shredded cheese, sour cream, and chopped green onions (optional).

Preparation:

1. In a skillet over medium heat, brown the ground beef, then drain excess fat.

2. Por the kidney beans, diced tomatoes, chopped onion, minced garlic, chilli powder, cumin, salt, and pepper to the crock pot with the cooked meat.

3. Now, cook for 6-8 hours on low or 3-4 hours on high. If feasible, stir occasionally.

4. If preferred, top the beef chilli with shredded cheese, sour cream, and chopped green onions.

These recipes provide a variety of tasty one-pot dinners that are easy to prepare and flavorful, making them ideal for individuals cooking for themselves and looking for hearty, satisfying foods.

CHAPTER 3

Easy Dinners

3.1 Lemon-Garlic Butter Salmon

Ingredients:

- 2 salmon fillets
- A quarter-cup of melted butter
- Two (2) tablespoons of lemon juice
- 2 minced garlic cloves
- Salt and pepper to taste
- Fresh parsley for garnish (optional)

Preparation:

1. Start by placing the salmon fillets in the slow cooker.

2. Combine the melted butter, lemon juice, minced garlic, salt, and pepper in a mixing bowl. Pour the mixture over the salmon.

3. Cook for 2-3 hours on low heat, or until the salmon is cooked through and flakes effortlessly with a fork.

4. Before serving, garnish with fresh parsley. Serve with roasted vegetables or rice.

3.2 Teriyaki Tofu Stir-Fry

Ingredients:

- 1 cubed block of tofu
- 1 cup chopped mixed veggies (such as bell peppers, broccoli, and carrots)
- A quarter-cup teriyaki sauce
- Two (2) tablespoons soy sauce
- 2 minced garlic cloves
- One (1) tablespoon sesame oil
- Serve with cooked rice or noodles.

Preparation:

1. In the crock pot, combine the cubed tofu and chopped vegetables.

2. Combine the teriyaki sauce, soy sauce, minced garlic, and sesame oil in a mixing bowl. Mixture should be poured over tofu and vegetables.

3. Cook for 2-3 hours on low, or until the tofu and vegetables are soft.

4. Serve the stir-fry teriyaki tofu over cooked rice or noodles.

3.3 Mexican Shredded Chicken

Ingredients:

- 1 pound skinless boneless chicken breasts
- 1 can diced tomatoes with green chilies (14 oz)
- One (1) chopped onion
- 2 minced garlic cloves
- Chili powder, two teaspoons
- 1 teaspoon cumin
- Season with salt and pepper to taste.
- Tortillas, lettuce, salsa, and other serving ingredients

Preparation:

1. Firstly, put the chicken breasts in the crock pot.

2. Add diced tomatoes, green chilies, chopped onion, minced garlic, chili powder, cumin, salt, and pepper.

3. Cook for 6-8 hours on low or 3-4 hours on high, or until the chicken is cooked and readily shreds.

4. Shred the chicken with two forks and combine it with the sauce in the crock pot.

5. Serve the Mexican shredded chicken in tortillas topped with lettuce, salsa, cheese, and sour cream.

3.4 Carnitas de porco

Ingredients:

- Two (2) pounds pork shoulder or pork butt, cut into chunks
- 1 chopped onion
- 4 minced garlic cloves
- One (1) teaspoon cumin
- One teaspoon of oregano
- One teaspoon of chili powder
- half a cup orange juice
- Serve with corn tortillas, cilantro, chopped onions and lime wedges.

Preparation:

1. Place the pork cubes in the crock pot.

2. Put in the onion, garlic, cumin, oregano, chili powder, and orange juice in a.

3. Cook for 8-10 hours on low or 4-6 hours on high, or until the pork is soft and readily shreds.

4. Shred the pork with two forks and combine it with the liquids in the slow cooker.

5. Serve the pork carnitas with cilantro, chopped onions and a squeeze of lime on corn tortillas.

3.5 Spaghetti Squash and Meatballs

Ingredients:

- One medium-sized spaghetti squash, halved & seeds removed
- 1 frozen pound meatballs
- 1 can marinara sauce (14 oz)
- A teaspoon of Italian seasoning
- Parmesan cheese, grated, for serving

Preparation:

1. Place the halved spaghetti squash, cut side up, in the crock pot.

2. Set up frozen meatballs around the squash.

3. Pour the marinara sauce over the meatballs and then sprinkle with Italian seasoning.

4. Cook on low for 6-7 hours or high for 3-4 hours, or until the squash is soft and the meatballs are well heated.

5. Scrape the squash into strands with a fork. Serve with meatballs, marinara sauce, and Parmesan cheese, if desired.

These dishes provide a variety of simple yet delicious supper options, making them ideal for folks looking for simple yet delicious meals for themselves.

CHAPTER 4

Sides and Extras

4.1 Garlic Mashed Potatoes

Ingredients:

- Four (4) big peeled and diced potatoes
- 4 minced garlic cloves
- 1/2 cup broth (chicken or veggie)
- 1/4 cup melted butter
- 1/4 cup heavy cream or milk
- Season with salt and pepper to taste.
- Optional garnish: chopped fresh parsley

Preparation:

1. In the crock pot, combine the cubed potatoes and minced garlic.

2. Add butter and chicken or veggie broth.

3. Cook for 6-7 hours on low or 3-4 hours on high, or until the potatoes are soft.

4. Mash the potatoes in the crock pot, gradually adding milk or heavy cream until the desired consistency is reached.

5. Before serving, season with salt and pepper and garnish with chopped fresh parsley.

4.2 Steamed Vegetables with Herb Butter

Ingredients:

- Assorted vegetables, chopped into florets or slices (broccoli, cauliflower, carrots, etc.)
- 1/4 cup melted butter
- 1 teaspoon dried herbs mixture (thyme, rosemary, oregano, etc.)
- Salt and pepper to taste

Preparation:

1. Place the vegetables in the crock pot.

2. Melt the butter in a small bowl and stir in the dried herbs.

3. Mix the herb butter with the veggies.

4. Cook for 2-3 hours on low, or until the vegetables are soft but still crisp.

5. Before serving, season with salt and pepper.

4.3 Quinoa Pilaf

Ingredients:

- 1 cup washed quinoa
- 2 cups broth (vegetable or chicken)
- 1 cup diced mixed veggies (such as bell peppers, peas, carrots, and so on)
- One teaspoon of olive oil
- Salt & pepper to taste
- Optional garnish: chopped fresh parsley

Preparation:

1. In the crock pot, combine the quinoa, broth, diced mixed veggies, and olive oil.

2. Cook on low for 2-3 hours or high for 1-2 hours, or until the quinoa is tender and the liquid has been absorbed.

3. Before serving, fluff the quinoa with a fork, season with salt and pepper, and garnish with chopped fresh parsley.

4.4 Mexican Rice

Ingredients:

- 1 cup white long-grain rice
- 1 can (14 oz.) chopped tomatoes with green chiles
- One (1) cup of broth (chicken or veggie)
- 1 tsp. chili powder
- A single teaspoon of cumin
- Salt to taste
- Optional garnish: chopped fresh cilantro

Preparation:

1. In the crock pot, combine the rice, diced tomatoes with green chilies, broth, chili powder, cumin, and salt.

2. Cook for 2-3 hours on low or 1-2 hours on high, until the rice is cooked and the liquid has been absorbed.

3. Before serving, fluff the rice with a fork and top with chopped fresh cilantro.

4.5 Creamy Mac and Cheese

Ingredients:

- Two (2) cups macaroni, uncooked
- 2 cups cheddar cheese, shredded
- 1 (12 oz) can evaporated milk
- 1/4 cup melted butter
- Optional: 1/2 teaspoon mustard powder

- Salt + pepper to taste

Preparation:

1. In the crock pot, combine the uncooked macaroni noodles, shredded cheddar cheese, evaporated milk, melted butter, mustard powder (if using), salt, and pepper.

2. Stir everything together thoroughly.

3. Cook, stirring regularly, for 2-3 hours on low, until the pasta is tender and the cheese has melted into a creamy sauce.

These side dishes and extras offer a variety of basic yet savoury options that can be served with main meals or as solo delights.

CHAPTER 5

Sweet Treats

5.1 Apple Cinnamon Oatmeal

Ingredients:

- 2 apples, peeled, cored, & chopped
- 1 cup rolled oats
- 2 cups milk (dairy or vegan)
- 2 tbsp. honey or maple syrup
- 1 teaspoon cinnamon
- Optional toppings: chopped nuts or raisins

Preparation:

1. In the crock pot, combine the diced apples, rolled oats, milk, honey or maple syrup, and cinnamon.

2. Stir everything together thoroughly.

3. Cook for 2-3 hours on low or 1-2 hours on high, until the oats are soft and the mixture has thickened.

4. If preferred, sprinkle with chopped nuts or raisins and serve warm.

5.2 Berry Cobbler

Ingredients:

- 4 cup berry mixture (strawberries, blueberries, raspberries)
- 1 cup regular flour
- 1 cup granulated sugar
- 1 tsp. baking powder
- 1/2 cup melted butter
- Vanilla ice cream or whipped cream (optional).

Preparation:

1. Fill the crock pot halfway with mixed berries.

2. In a mixing dish, combine the flour, sugar, and baking powder.

3. Add the melted butter and stir until the mixture resembles coarse crumbs.

4. Spread the flour mixture over the berries in the crock pot.

5. Cook for 2-3 hours on low heat, or until the topping is golden brown and the berries are bubbly.

6. Serve the warm berry cobbler with vanilla ice cream or whipped cream, if desired.

5.3 Rice Pudding

Ingredients:

- 1 cup white rice
- 4 cups milk (dairy or vegan)
- 1/2 cup granulated sugar
- A tsp vanilla extract
- 1/2 teaspoon ground cinnamon
- Optional garnish: raisins or chopped nuts

Preparation:

1. Drain the white rice after rinsing it in cool water.

2. In the crock pot, combine the rinsed rice, milk, sugar, vanilla extract, and ground cinnamon.

3. Stir everything together thoroughly.

4. Cook for 3-4 hours on low or 1-2 hours on high, until the rice is cooked and the mixture thickens.

5. While cooking, stir the rice pudding occasionally.

6. If desired, serve the rice pudding warm or cooled, garnished with raisins or chopped nuts.

5.4 Chocolate Lava Cake

Ingredients:

- 1 cup regular flour
- 1/2 cup granulated sugar
- 1/4 cup cocoa powder, unsweetened
- 1 tsp. baking powder
- A quarter teaspoon of salt
- 1/2 cup milk (dairy or vegan)
- 2 tbsp. softened butter
- A tsp vanilla extract
- 3/4 cup brown sugar, packed
- 1/4 cup cocoa powder, unsweetened
- 1+3/4 cup boiling water

Preparation:

1. Combine the flour, granulated sugar, 1/4 cup cocoa powder, baking powder, and salt in a mixing basin/bowl.

2. Add in the milk, melted butter, and vanilla extract until blended.

3. Spread the mixture evenly in the crock pot's bottom.

4. In a separate bowl, combine the brown sugar and the remaining 1/4 cup cocoa powder.

5. Sprinkle the brown sugar-cocoa mixture on top of the batter in the crock pot.

6. At this point, pour hot water over the top without stirring.

7. Cook the cake on high for 2-3 hours, or until the borders are firm but the centre is still mushy.

8. If desired, serve the chocolate lava cake warm, topped with ice cream or whipped cream.

5.5 Peach Crisp

Ingredients:

- 4 cups peaches, sliced (fresh or canned)
- 1 cup rolled oats, old-fashioned
- 1/2 cup regular flour
- 1/2 cup brown sugar, packed
- 1/4 cup granulated sugar
- 1 teaspoon ground cinnamon
- 1/2 cup melted butter
- Optional vanilla ice cream for serve

Preparation:

1. Put the sliced peaches in the bottom of the crock pot.

2. Combine the rolled oats, flour, brown sugar, granulated sugar, cinnamon, and melted butter in a mixing bowl until crumbly.

3. Distribute the oat mixture evenly over the peaches in the crock pot.

4. Cook for 3-4 hours on low heat, or until the peaches are soft and the topping is golden brown.

5. Serve the peach crisp warm, with vanilla ice cream on top if preferred.

These sweet treat recipes provide delectable options for satisfying dessert cravings with minimal effort, making them ideal for individuals who cook for themselves or seek easy yet decadent desserts.

CHAPTER 6

Your 14-day Meal Plan

Here's a 14-day meal plan based on the recipes provided in this book, incorporating a variety of soups, one-pot meals, easy dinners, sides, and sweet treats:

Day 1:
Lunch: Hearty Chicken Noodle Soup (Chapter 1)
Dinner: BBQ Pulled Pork Sandwiches (Chapter 2)

Day 2:
Lunch: Lentil and Tomato Soup (Chapter 1)
Dinner: Italian Sausage with Peppers (Chapter 2)

Day 3:
Lunch: Creamy Potato Soup (Chapter 1)
Dinner: Lemon-Garlic Butter Salmon (Chapter 3)

Day 4:
Lunch: Split Pea Soup (Chapter 1)
Dinner: Teriyaki Tofu Stir-Fry (Chapter 3)

Day 5:
Lunch: Beef and Vegetable Stew (Chapter 1)
Dinner: Mexican Shredded Chicken Tacos (Chapter 3)

Day 6:
Lunch: Veggie Ratatouille (Chapter 2)
Dinner: Pork Carnitas Tacos (Chapter 3)

Day 7:
Lunch: Quinoa Pilaf (Chapter 4)
Dinner: Spaghetti Squash and Meatballs (Chapter 3)

Day 8:
Lunch: Steamed Vegetables with Herb Butter (Chapter 4)
Dinner: Beef Chili (Chapter 2)

Day 9:
Lunch: Mexican Rice (Chapter 4)
Dinner: Honey Garlic Chicken (Chapter 2)

Day 10:
Lunch: Creamy Mac and Cheese (Chapter 4)
Dinner: Berry Cobbler (Chapter 5)

Day 11:
Lunch: Garlic Mashed Potatoes (Chapter 4)
Dinner: Apple Cinnamon Oatmeal (Chapter 5)

Day 12:
Lunch: Rice Pudding (Chapter 5)
Dinner: Peach Crisp (Chapter 5)

Day 13:
Lunch: Lemon-Garlic Butter Salmon (Chapter 3)
Dinner: BBQ Pulled Pork Sandwiches (Chapter 2)

Day 14:

Lunch: Split Pea Soup (Chapter 1)
Dinner: Chocolate Lava Cake (Chapter 5)

Enjoy your delicious and diverse 14-day meal plan!

CHAPTER 7

Crock Pot Cooking Hacks for Singles

1. Maximizing Leftovers: Creative Ways to Repurpose Meals

- Plan meals that provide flexible leftovers, such as roasted meats that may be transformed into sandwiches, salads, or wraps for the next day's lunch.

- Freeze for Future Feasts: Freeze extra portions in single-serving containers for quick and convenient meals on busy days.
-

2. Freezing Tips: Storing and Reheating Crock Pot Meals

- Individual Portions: Freeze leftovers in single servings for quick grab-and-go meals.

- Labelling Containers Properly: Label containers with dates and meal titles to keep track of what's in the freezer.

- Safe Thawing: Defrost meals in the fridge overnight or use the microwave for quick defrosting before reheating.

3. Batch Cooking: Streamlining Meal Prep for the Week Ahead

- Cook Once, Eat Many Times: Prepare a large batch of a versatile dish like soup, stew, or curry to enjoy for the rest of the week.

- Variety is Key: To add diversity to your meals, modify the flavours or add various sides.

4. Ingredient Substitutions: Making the Most with What You Have

- Ingredient Flexibility: Learn to substitute ingredients to accommodate what's in your cupboard or fridge without compromising taste.

- Adapt and Conquer: To make recipes more appealing to your taste, modify them depending on personal tastes or dietary requirements.

5. Time-Saving Strategies: Overnight Cooking and Meal Planning

- Overnight Magic: Use the crock pot's "low" setting for overnight cooking to wake up to a freshly made breakfast or ready-to-eat lunch.

- Benefits of Meal Planning: Devote a little amount of time each week to meal planning, making grocery shopping and meal prep more efficient.

6. Cleaning and Maintenance Tips

- To make cleaning the crock pot easier, use liners or nonstick cooking spray.

- Cleaning and maintaining your crock pot on a regular basis will keep it in good shape and ready to use.

7. Portion Control and Storage Solutions

- To avoid overeating, adjust recipes to fit your portion needs or freeze leftovers right away.

- Compact Storage: To save room in a tiny kitchen, choose smaller-sized crock pots or multi-purpose kitchen gadgets.

These crock pot cooking hacks are intended to help folks cooking for themselves expedite meal preparation, maximise ingredients, and make the cooking experience more efficient and enjoyable.

CONCLUSION

Embracing Effortless and Flavorful Cooking for Singles

Cooking for one does not have to mean forfeiting flavour, diversity, or ease of preparation. With the right tools & techniques, the crock pot becomes a steadfast companion in your culinary journey, providing simplicity, versatility, and delightful meals.

In this cookbook, we've explored the amazing possibilities of crock pot cooking tailored specifically for singles. Each meal, from easy 5-ingredient recipes to hearty soups, one-pot miracles, sides, and sweet pleasures, is designed to minimise work while maximising flavour.

Furthermore, the useful ideas, techniques, and strategies presented enable you to easily manage your kitchen. Repurposing leftovers, mastering batch cooking, and customising recipes to your tastes become second nature, allowing you to enjoy wonderful meals without the burden of lengthy preparation.

Cooking for yourself is a kind of self-care and creativity. It's about embracing flavours, experimenting with ingredients, and savouring the pleasure that comes with each bite.

So, fire up your slow cooker, experiment with these recipes, and start on a culinary adventure that celebrates the simplicity and richness of meals made just for you. Here's to cooking that's simple, joyful, and satisfying—bon appétit!

Happy cooking,

Bell Quintana

My Little Request

Thank You For Reading This Book!
I really appreciate all of your feedback and
I love to hear what you have to say.

I need your input to make the next version of this
book and my future books better.

Please take two minutes now to leave a helpful review on
Amazon letting me know what you thought of the book:
Thanks so much!
Bell Quintana

NOTES

(For Your Favorite Recipes or Notes)

Attribution

All images used in this book were downloaded from *pexels.com.*

Made in United States
Troutdale, OR
02/23/2024

17860818R00037